Chants *of* Life!

Designed & Produced
by
Wilbek & Lewbar
90 Victoria Road, Devizes
Wiltshire, SN10 1EU

Author Sister Hannah Elizabeth CCC
Editor Bob Wilson
Illustrations Ossie Jones
Design & Layout Greenland Design Ltd

Printed in Great Britain

This book is dedicated to:
all those who have touched my life,
and thus added a note or notes
to the Eternal Chant.

Contents

INTRODUCTION

During our journey through life we often find ourselves standing at a crossroad. Each crossroad can represent all manner of things, some good, some bad, some of no consequence whatsoever.

One of my crossroads led to a meeting with the authoress of this book of illustrated poetry, Sister Hannah. This being my very first meeting with a lady of the cloth, I was very unsure as to where it would lead. The moment we met I became instantly captivated by this lady's zest for life, her incredibly wicked sense of humour and tremendous strength of Faith.

Sister Hannah has a rare progressive neurological disease but has no time for illness. Her high speed life is devoted to helping others, giving warmth, comfort and guidance. Her inner strength and wicked humour making light of all obstacles, winning over all she meets.

In reading through the pages of this book I hope you will also then carry a little part of Sister Hannah in your heart!

Bob Wilson
Editor

Scatterbrain

I'm really so forgetful,
I am quite scatterbrained.
On my desk there lies a memo-pad -
To get my memory trained.

I'd be lost without a diary:
It's a vital daily guide.
It reminds me of appointments -
If I remember to look inside!

It's really quite a problem:
Did I wash one arm or more?
Perhaps I'll do them both again
For then I shall be sure!

Once - after having my hair done -
I was looking along the line
To find the coat I thought I'd worn,
But forgot which one was mine!

Another time it was even worse,
Though it caused us so much laughter,
For I returned in SOMEONE ELSE'S coat
(Which Mum discovered after).

Some keys were in the pocket,
But what we couldn't figure
Was how I hadn't noticed
It was several sizes bigger.

At The 'Chippy'

Whilst queuing at the chippy,
I felt a little nippy.
I also thought it rather odd
That when I asked for battered cod,
There went up such a loud, long laugh,
With looks exchanged between the staff.

What was so funny? I asked myself -
Until I looked upon the shelf -
To see a notice plain as plain
The new arrangements to explain!
I'd wandered in without a thought:
I didn't know the shop was bought!

I stood there feeling really daft
While everyone else just laughed and laughed.
The Manager told me with utmost grace
That today they had no cod or plaice -
"We have some sole but it's rather tough
Because it's made of leather stuff!"

The chippy that I'd known so long
Dealt now not with fish but with last and thong,
For the sole to which the man had referred
Was at base of shoe which had just been repaired!
So next time you go to buy bangers and chop -
Make sure that you're standing in the right shop!

NEWS

The Fruit and the Spirit

You have heard of itinerant preachers;
Well here's something quite unique -
For Sheila shares the Love of the Lord
As she weighs up the carrots and leek.

Yes, Sheila has a travelling van
From which she sells veg and fresh fruit,
And she freely brings fruit of the spiritual kind
As well as the beans and beetroot!

As she weighs up the apples and onions,
She always readily shares.
She offers a word to encourage
As she bags up the plums and the pears.

So if you are needing potatoes -
Or maybe some turnip or swede -
Why don't you buy them from Sheila's van
For she also brings spiritual seed:

The seed of the fruit of the Spirit -
Of Love and Joy and Peace -
She'll tell you how these seeds can grow
And gradually increase.

We thank the Lord for Sheila's van,
For her ministry week by week,
For through her travelling fruit and veg
The Lord can surely speak!

Nobody's Perfect

No doubt we have all - at some time or other -
Looked in the mirror to discover
That some things are not as we'd like them to be,
(If I had the chance I'd change bits of me)!

But please consider, if you will,
The problem that is facing Jill,
For she always looks so trim and neat
Until you see her gigantic feet.

And then there's the case of Angela Rose,
Who suffers because of her oversized nose;
And in the winter - try as she will -
Her nose is the first part to feel the chill.

And have you heard about poor young Peers?
He has a problem with sticking out ears!
He's the victim of so much ridicule
And it's been the same since he went to school.

I've also heard about Monica Grace
Who feels that she has too square a face.
"It's very hard", she says with a frown,
"To discover a way to narrow it down"!

But by contrast, Mrs. Theresa Flynn
Has trouble with a pointed chin.
But none of these flaws will do us harm
And beauty is not as important as charm.

Tongue in Cheek

In considering the Clergy, it's very plain to see,
That though they're only human - just like you 'n' me -
We place upon them great demands
And think they'll jump to our commands.

But surely we - the laity -
Should accept responsibility,
And give the Vicar our loyal backing
For there's much in us that's lacking.

We're always ready with criticism
If he overdoes the witticism ...
Yet there are those who would not hide
The fact that they like his humorous side.

The Vicar's job is full of tension;
He wonders if there will be dissension,
For it's a tricky situation
Explaining to the congregation ...

That "As from next month there will be a change,
For we really must explore the range
Of Worship material, old and new,
So that we hold a balanced view".

With all this stress it's no small wonder
That he rarely makes a blunder;
So I can say (with tongue in cheek!)
Who'd blame him for working
Just ONE DAY A WEEK?

HYMNS
432
19
389
9

Eavesdropping

Whilst waiting at the surgery
It's quite an education
To just sit very quietly
And catch the conversation;
For if you listen carefully
Then possibly you can
Learn of every operation
Available to man!

One woman is explaining of her massive blood transfusion,
And how (all because of her)
The ward was in confusion!
At last the doctor calls you in -
Your face shows disappointment,
For had he been a minute late
You'd have heard the next instalment.

The Landlady

A landlady's life is a busy one,
From early morn 'til the setting sun,
For the guests must always feel at home
In her guest house called The Hippodrome.

The good reputation must be kept:
Some people of note in this house have slept,
And now some new people are expected
The state of the rooms must again be inspected.

The landlady brings fresh sheets for the bed
Then orders the extra milk and bread.
Her gift is hospitality:
There's a sense of informality ...

And it comes as no surprise to learn
That all her guests will soon return.

Beautiful Garden

When you wake in the morning, what do you see?
There's so much beauty for you - and for me!

As you stir in your bed at the break of the day,
The garden wakes, too, in its own special way:
Flowers lift their heads to the rising sun,
Birds sing in chorus - a new day has begun.

Outside my window, anchored to the hedge,
Fine lace of the humble spider's web -
A wheel of silver spokes I see -
Worked while I was still abed.

As the evening comes and the darkness falls,
Birds sing out their good night calls,
Flower heads droop and petals close -
From anemones to the Regal rose.

As in the house the curtains are drawn,
The sun sets on a velvet lawn...

...And another day is done.

Money-go-Round

Money is always in demand,
Being passed from hand to hand.

From the largest note to the halfpenny small,
Just what are they but tokens all?

Then why this quest for more and more?
Let's stop this greed and consider the poor!

Let's spare a thought for those who are needy,
Share our resources and cease being greedy.

Bring back the Small Shops

Things today it seems are vast;
The personal touch is a thing of the past;
Gone the days of the customer's chair,
And assistants in stores don't seem to care.

Bring back the small shops, those were the days,
Stores to me are one big maze.
No friendly faces to help you choose,
And no friendly chatter while you muse.

Big shops, it seems, are in the rat race,
So bring back the small shops and slacken the pace,
Then you can choose your goods at leisure -
Shopping will once more become a pleasure.

In the Park

A woman is feeding the ducks on the pond
And there's tennis in progress just beyond;
Children are playing on swings and slides,
And oh how gently the roundabout glides
And it's all in the park.

Women with prams giving baby fresh air,
And children with nannies - some with grey hair.
There are signs here and there saying "Keep off the grass",
But there's plenty of room on the path to pass,
And it's all in the park.

There are shady trees and a place to sit -
I love to come to the park for a bit.
So if I have an hour to spare,
Be sure that you will find me there.

Spectator on Wheels

I'm a spectator -just like you,
But I watch MY sport from a different view:
Not for me a stand, way up there -
For my seat comes with me - it's my wheelchair!

In some sports I can participate:
In table-tennis and swimming.
The important thing is to be like you;
I really don't mind about winning.

For others like me I would make a plea -
To the planners this thing I would stress:
So that our favourite sport we can see -
PLEASE be sure we have access!

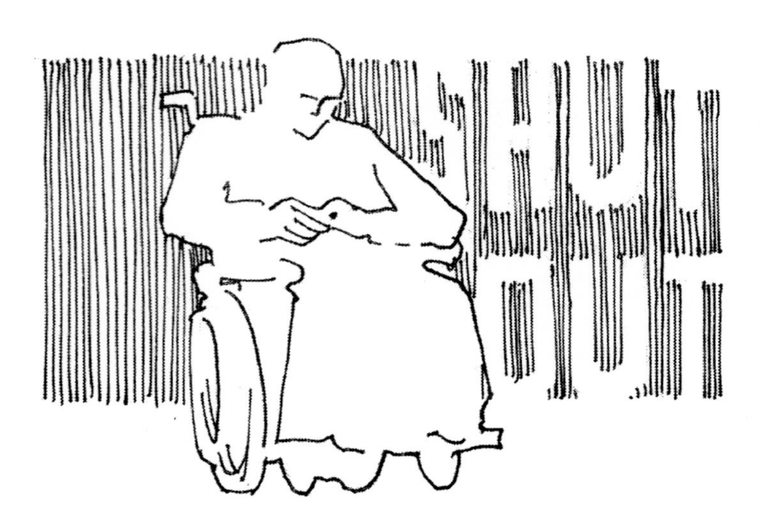

True Friendship

It's good to have a friend that's true
And such a one is surely you!
My worries and my joys I share,
Knowing that you really care.

Always helpful, always kind,
Good friends like you are hard to find;
To my faults you seem immune,
And when we talk, we are in tune.

There's little more that I can say,
Remembering you always when I pray
At evening when the day is through,
I thank the Lord for a friend like you.

Winter Evening

Draw the curtains, switch on the light,
Pull up a chair by the fire;
Relax a while when the night draws in
As you watch the flames leap higher.

When the embers glow and the moon shines bright,
Then is the time to retire;
So close your eyes and sleep will come
And dream of your heart's desire.

As you prepare yourself for rest
The wise old owl awakes -
And when in the morning you rise from your bed
Then he his rest will take.

Sleep well my friend, but spare a thought
For those who work at night -
Those who brave the winter chills,
Who work by the moonshine bright.

Those who guard us, those who feed us,
Those who print the news;
Doctors, nurses, those who serve us -
They all deserve their dues.

Remember too, the folk who travel
By road, rail, air or sea;
Those who tramp along the highway,
Maybe sleeping ,neath a tree.

May God be with them, one and all,
May they claim the Lord's protection;
Seek His blessed company
And ask him for direction.

These Things are Life

The miracle I saw today,
I'll see again tomorrow,
The dawn that follows the darkest night.
The joy that comes after sorrow.
These things are Life

Flora, fauna, starry skies
The song of a bird or a laughing child.
Busy cities, wide open spaces,
So many things to delight our eyes.
These things are Life

A challenge faced,
A battle won,
Problems overcome.
Relaxing when our work is done,
Security, a happy home.
These things are Life

From failure springs success
And we must learn from our mistakes.
Courage and a spirit brave,
Courage friend, that's what it takes.
For this is Life

Showers and sunshine, tears and smiles,
A friend to help us on our way,
A "thank you" that makes things so worthwhile.
These things are Life

Sleeping, working, singing and playing,
Genesis, growth, development,
Thank you Lord my heart is saying.
For this is Life

Springtime Walk

This afternoon we went for a walk.
With an elderly lady stopped to talk
And admired her lilac tree.
As we chatted she stretched and cut,
And soon there was a bunch for me.

We continued on our way,
Past gardens where with up-turned faces,
Gentle pansies smiled at me.
Whilst high above on roof and tree
The blackbird sang his praises.

Lord, thank you for the beauty in creation
which I saw this very day
For the clear blue sky and sun that shone
To warm us with his rays.

Then pour your Holy Spirit Lord deep into my heart
That in praising my Creator I may play my part.
Amen.

A Baby on the Way

I was so happy to hear you say:
"We have a baby on the way"!

I can understand your joy
At the thought of a girl or boy
To share your home, your life - your LOVE!

I'm sure your Mum's just over the moon
To think she'll be a Grandma soon.

Tiny feet and tiny hands
Will all be part of your future plans

And I hope and pray when babe comes along
he'll be happy and bonny, healthy and strong;

And I hope as well on OUR door you will tap
and place the baby in my lap.

Magic Carpet

If you have to stay in bed
and find it rather a bore,
then enter the realm of make believe
and on a Magic Carpet soar.

Above the clouds of grey despair,
up into the clear, clear air.

Then on the wings of imagination
reach your chosen destination;
over the ocean or down the street,
for with a Magic Carpet the whole world's at your feet.

So if you're lying on your back
and you don't much like the view:
Into a case your troubles pack -
the rest is up to you!

To a Rocking Chair

Old rocking chair,
I wonder-
Although you're dusty, threadbare -
What tales you have to tell?

What characters into sweet dreams
have you lulled?
Let me close my eyes and imagine...

...Ah yes -
The little old man
Who smoked a pipe;

A white - haired old lady
With shoulders bent;
Hiding inside her crocheted shawl,
Gently into sleep you sent
As you rocked back and forth
By a roaring fire.

You are aged now; in a corner you stay -
Though there's life in you yet!
And I'd like to think folk don't forget
The comfort you gave in some bygone day.

Maybe a happy ghost will come
To visit you when day is done.

On the Highway

If on the highway you would travel
there is a code you must unravel:
For if you're a user of the road
You must obey the Highway Code.

Take care to learn the warning signs
and don't cross over double white lines.
For if you're a user of the road
You must obey the Highway Code.

When you see warnings, mostly triangular
and directions, mostly rectangular,
Remember, user of the road
You must obey the Highway Code.

Lines and lanes are there to guide you,
in holdups do not jump the queue;
Give way to pedestrians on the crossing
and out of the window no litter tossing.
For if you're a user of the road
You must obey the Highway Code.

If you are walking out at night
please be seen and wear something light.
With great care approach the junctions;
wardens and lights all have their functions.

So for the safety of the road
please obey the Highway Code.

You must not lead an animal if you're on your bike;
unless you have a seat to do so, don't give lifts to those who hike.
For if you're a user of the road
You must obey the Highway Code.

In your mirror keep in view
the traffic that is following you;
be sure your signals are always clear
that all may proceed with nothing to fear.

So if you're a user of the road,
you must obey the Highway Code.

If you've already passed your test
then keep your standard at its best
And when you've passed the exam of the road
please don't FORGET the Highway Code.

Whether You ride or cycle or drive
OBEY THE CODE AND STAY ALIVE!

You Hold the Key

Your heart is sad you see through mist-

In times of darkness, isolation,
Search your store of memories.
Surely you'll find consolation
And 'tis you my friend who holds the keys
To courage for the future;
Keys of hope for days to come.

Hold on then in your days of sorrow
From your store of memories borrow.
Be sure that sun will follow shadow
Look o'er yonder towards that rainbow.

Mercy Dash

There's been a very nasty crash -
the ambulance goes on a mercy dash.

On the site first-aid is given,
then the casualties are driven
to the hospital at top speed,
where there are experts to meet the need.

Those angels in green and blue and white
are a very reassuring sight.

I could easily write a screed
on kindly word and gentle deed.
Suffice it to say when you're not so scared
You will be thankful for those who cared.

Hospital Experience

The trolley rumbled down the ward
and stopped right by my bed -
there must be some mistake, I thought-
I'd not had my pre-med.

Down to Theatre Number 2,
well there's not much now that I can do.
"It will soon be over, you won't feel a thing" -
words with a somewhat familiar ring!

The anaesthetist was very charming -
his injection was disarming!
My head starts spinning,
I know no more
Till I wake up and feel very sore!

"You're back in the ward, dear,
All is well"
My goodness, there's the visitor's bell-
Have I been sleeping for all that time?
To waste it would surely be a crime-
But this is healing sleep I know—
from Him from whom ALL BLESSINGS FLOW

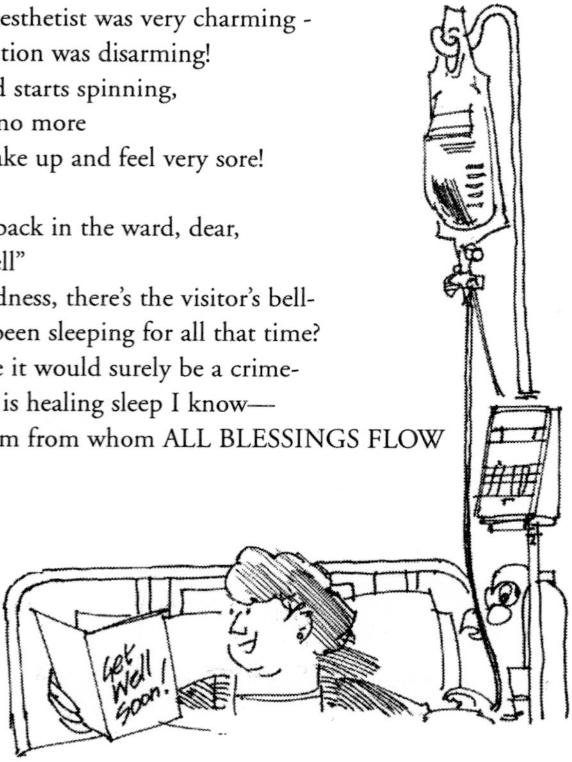

Colours of December

Looking from my window one bleak December day;
I realised of a sudden
That things were not so grey:
Red Robin chirped, the sun came through -
The sky above was streaked with blue
And gone, once more, the pure white snow.

Soon, I thought, the Christmas lights
Would brighten up the shops;
Whilst in my garden-on the lawn -
My friend, Red Robin, hops.

Green trees bedecked with silver, gold
(Who knows what those parcels hold)?
Parcels of every shape and size,
Eagerly viewed through wide, bright eyes.

On Christmas Eve the stockings are hung
Above the fire, and Carols sung.
In the still night air the Church bells ring
And we remember the gift of JESUS OUR KING.

Christingle

In a country called Moravia many years ago,
Was the first Christingle service,
Jesu's Love to show.

Symbols of the love of the world,
The blood of Christ; the fruits of the earth;
These things with the voices of children mingle
At the service of Christingle.

Somewhere a child needing special care
Will receive the gifts of those who share
In the colourful service of Christingle.

The spirit of Christmas -
A loving deed -
Children giving for children in need.

Just Like You

I'm NOT "Fragile-handle with care!"
Because I'm in a wheelchair.
Then why regard me as you do?
Can't you see? I'm just like YOU!

When reading a letter I'd written,
Or talking on the phone -
Unless you had met me face to face -
Is it not true you might NEVER HAVE KNOWN ?

Yet you seem to be embarrassed
If you meet me in the street.
Why can't you just ACCEPT ME?
It'd make my day complete!

You talk down to me, as if to a child,
Or whisper, "Poor thing, what a shame."
Be tolerant, have patience
And learn to play the game.

For as a member of SOCIETY have I not the right
To prove my own ability - to be equal in your sight?

Please give me a chance - that's all I ask-
You shouldn't have too hard a task.

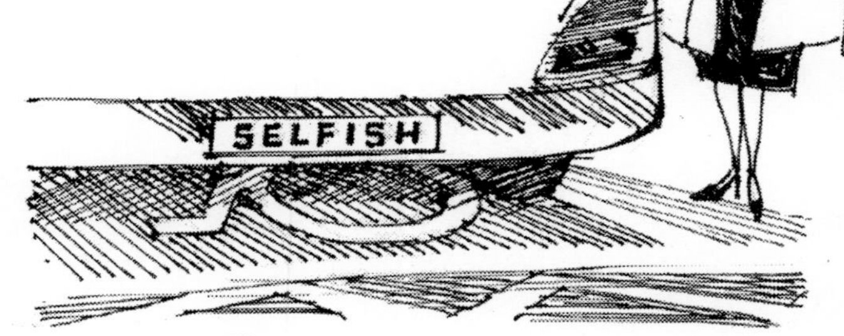

The Rescue!

I tried to smile and not to frown -
The night me through floor lift broke down ...

I were actually on me way t' bed
When suddenly the lift stopped dead!

I tried all sorts to get it going,
But the mechanical juices were clearly not flowing.

Next I rang the Service Department -
I think the girl had an empty compartment!

She asked: 'D'you want someone there tonight?'
I could do nothing but sit quite tight

And wait for the engineer to ring -
But when he did, 't'weren't good news to bring

For'e were stuck in Cheltenham Spa -
T'would take him long to get that far.

Meanwhile I waited midway between floors
With Maria unable to finish her chores.

Me 'ead was in the bedroom,
Me legs were in the lounge...

And then I got a bit thirsty
So Maria went on the scrounge -

She raided the fridge for lemonade (and chocolate)
And then I was told: 'Ring the Fire Brigade';

Reluctantly dialling '999'
Six men arrived in record time!

They soon had the lift back down to the ground -
I was so relieved - and joy did abound,

But wait ... I needed to be upstairs...
I wanted to sleep with my teddy bears!
Well two of the six very trusty crew
Took it all in their stride; knew just what to do!

Thank God for all who rush to my aid -
And three cheers for the Corsham Fire Brigade!

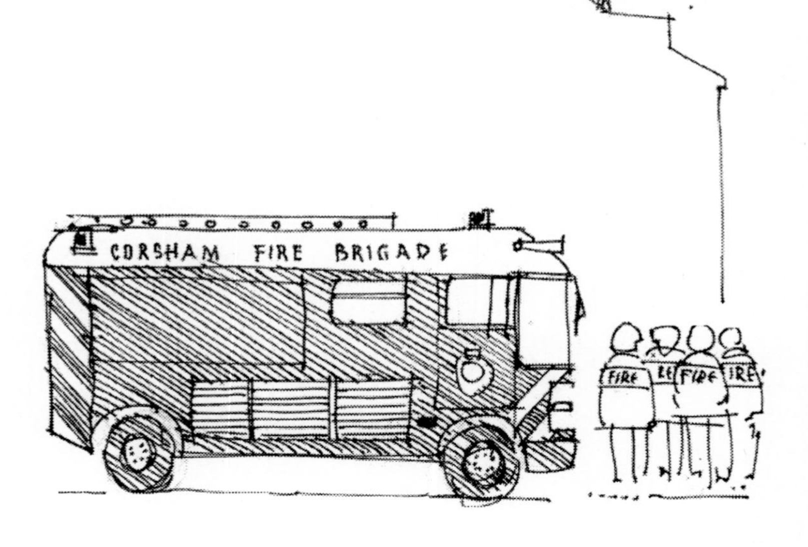

What Can I Eat?

I can't eat white bread
She can't eat brown;
Me teeth don't like toffees -
They stick to me crown.

We've cut down on sugar
And salt and grease,
Or else 'they' say
We'll be very obese;

Too much of the butter
Is bad for cholesterol
But 'alf my problems are
Purely ancestral!

Me mother was fat,
Me father, too
And they were both partial
To dumplings and stew!

Now beef has been banned
From our table for years
And gone are the eggs
(Salmonella fears).

The chocolate's reduced -
Now that's very sad:
I'm quite sure that everything nice
Can't be bad.

I do like me chips
And nobody's stoppin'
Me adding a portion
To Friday's shoppin'.

I know that over-use
Of the griddle
May result in
An oversize middle!

Directives from Brussels
Can leave me confused -
Why grow straight bananas?
I am so bemused!

Why should I change
My eating habits?
They'll turn us into
A nation of rabbits!

Telling us what to eat and why
Can lead to much frustration:
What you fancy does you good -
But of course in moderation!

His World - A Room

You're bored you say -
Nothing to do, nowhere to go;
You're tired of this and don't like that.

Yet, surely, you have much to thank God for -
A sound mind and healthy body...

Then please spare a thought
For one whose WORLD became just
One SMALL ROOM.

One Small room, which (beside bed and chair)
Was filled to capacity with treasures
Evoking love, and happy memories -

Yes, happy memories - not bitter-
Of the days when he was stronger.
When some of the common activities
Came within his reach.

Then, as the years passed
And he gradually weakened,
Did he grow miserable?

Certainly not! Ever cheerful,
Ever smiling-though he was now too weak
To feed himself - with the courage of a
Martyr and the patience of a Saint.
He faced each day in the same way-
Until the end,

Now his struggle is over -
The victory is his
And his reward is PEACE.

Old was he? Not so,
For he was less than twenty when he died:

But he has left us with
No mean legacy -
A shining example
So PLEASE spare a thought
For the one whose world became
Just ONE SMALL ROOM.

My Teddy

I've had my Teddy for years and years -
I tell him all my joys and fears.
He stays with me when I'm ill in bed:
A really good friend it must be said.

Poor Teddy is showing signs of wear -
His stuffing is showing here and there,
He's had operations and stitches, too -
But I'd rather have HIM than one that's new!

Beside me each night my Teddy sleeps,
And all my secrets he faithfully keeps;
Then when I awake dear Teddy is there,
I just wouldn't be without my bear!

The Dieter

I really must try that bit harder
To resist what's in the larder!
No secret nibbles behind closed doors,
For that's what the dietitian abhors!

It's all very well saying "Just cut down",
But every time I go to town
I have to pass the bakery -
And oh! how I'd love a cream cake for tea!

I've never been one for steak and chips,
But I just cannot get to grips
With this business of counting the calories:
How many in bread or a piece of cheese?

But the thought of the holiday spurs me on,
For I've bought a new dress I'd like to don -

And on that score I think I've been rather clever
In buying a size that I'd normally NEVER
Be able to wear in my present state -
So you see I've just got to lose some weight!

Other Books By Writer

1. Good Morning Lord (prayers & meditations)
2. On My Mind (poetry)
3. Thank you Lord (prayers & meditations)
4. Butterflies And Rainbows (modern parables)
5. With Tongue In Cheek (humorous poetry)
6. Miscellany Of Poems And Reflections (poetry)
7. Travelling On Together (Christian songs/music to accompany tape)
8. These Things Are Life (poetry)
9. Come Lord Jesus (Advent Meditations)
10. In His Strength (autobiography 'part one')

Wilbek & Lewbar
Publishers
90 Victoria Road
Devizes
Wiltshire
SN10 1EU
Tel No 01380 720271
E-mail wil.bar@zetnet.co.uk